YOU'RE OVER THE HILL WHEN...

Written by
HERB KAVET

Designed and Illustrated by
MARTY RISKIN

COPYRIGHT 1991

IVORY TOWER PUBLISHING COMPANY INCORPORATED

PUBLISHED SIMULTANEOUSLY IN CANADA BY MARKA CANADA ETOBICOKE, ONTARIO M9W 5Z6

DISTRIBUTED IN THE UNITED KINGDOM BY AZLON LONDON LTD., LONDON SW11 3UP & WHYNOT PRODUCTIONS LTD. EAST SUSSEX TN21 0XL

DISTRIBUTED IN AUSTRALIA BY ABALNON PTY. LTD. CONCORD WEST, N.S.W. 2138

DISTRIBUTED IN NEW ZEALAND BY BLACKWOOD GAYLE DISTRIBUTORS AUCKLAND.

IVORY TOWER PUBLISHING COMPANY, INC.
125 WALNUT STREET, WATERTOWN, MA 02172
TEL#: (617) 923-1111
FAX: (617) 923-8839

YOU'RE OVER THE HILL WHEN...

You see your old cereal bowl
in an antique shop.

YOU'RE OVER THE HILL WHEN...

You meet old friends
and you tell each other
"YOU HAVEN'T CHANGED A BIT."

YOU'RE OVER THE HILL WHEN...

Your name appears on every mail order list in the country.

Getting a little action
means your prune juice is working.

You still feel your youthful ardor,
but only once in a while.

YOU'RE
OVER THE HILL
WHEN...

You have a very special comfortable chair
from which it is very difficult
to remove you.

YOU'RE
OVER THE HILL
WHEN...

Your arms are barely long enough
to hold your reading material.

A hair on your head is worth 2
in the brush.

YOU'RE OVER THE HILL WHEN...

Your stomach gets upset if you eat raw cookie dough.

YOU'RE OVER THE HILL WHEN...

You add "God Willing"
to the end of most of your statements.

YOU'RE OVER THE HILL WHEN...

You recognize that middle age spread only serves to bring people closer together.

You're smart enough not to take out
all the garbage in one trip.

YOU'RE OVER THE HILL WHEN...

You no longer brag about how many parking tickets you have.

You never owned edible underwear.

There are no longer cartoons and report cards on your refrigerator door.

YOU'RE
OVER THE HILL
WHEN...

You remember to stop the newspapers before going on vacation.

YOU'RE
OVER THE HILL
WHEN...

You never run out of toilet paper.

YOU'RE OVER THE HILL WHEN...

You feel most comfortable straddling two lanes.

You don't go to nude beaches.

YOU'RE
OVER THE HILL
WHEN...

You look at the menu before looking at
the waitress or waiter.

YOU'RE OVER THE HILL WHEN...

You always pay your phone and electric bills before they are due.

YOU'RE OVER THE HILL WHEN...

You start dressing for comfort.
Your color coordination takes a back seat
to expediency.

YOU'RE OVER THE HILL WHEN...

You actually read most of the magazines you have subscriptions to.

YOU'RE
OVER THE HILL
WHEN...

You no longer apologize for your gay
or weird friends.

YOU'RE OVER THE HILL WHEN...

No one cares anymore about what you did in high school.

YOU'RE
OVER THE HILL
WHEN...

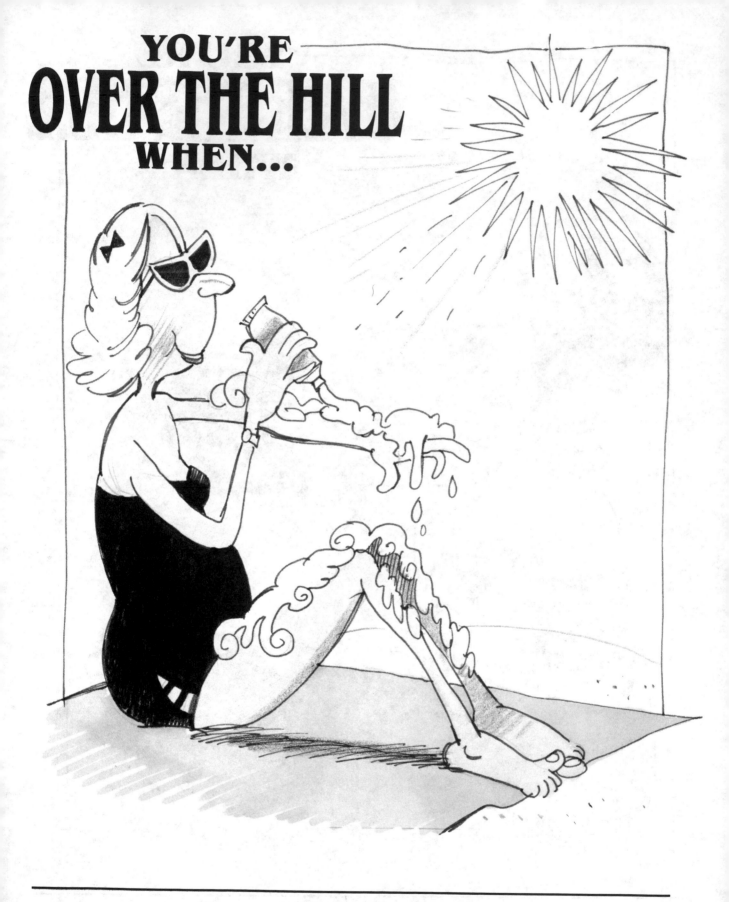

You worry about the
long term effect of the sun on your skin,
but still love a tan.

YOU'RE OVER THE HILL WHEN...

You find yourself squinting during candlelight dinners.

YOU'RE
OVER THE HILL
WHEN...

You are resigned to the fact
that certain foods just aren't compatible
with your gastrointestinal system.

YOU'RE OVER THE HILL WHEN...

You start looking forward to dull evenings at home.

YOU'RE OVER THE HILL WHEN...

You're resigned to being slightly overweight after trying every diet that has come along in the last 15 years.

YOU'RE OVER THE HILL WHEN...

Pretty much everything you own is paid for. You can finally afford lots of things that you no longer want.

YOU'RE OVER THE HILL WHEN...

You feel like the morning after and you can swear you haven't been anywhere.

YOU'RE OVER THE HILL WHEN...

You sit down to put on your underwear. Other people have brightly colored shorts but yours are all white.

YOU'RE
OVER THE HILL
WHEN...

You no longer throw out
your too wide or too narrow neckties,
knowing they will eventually
come back into style.

YOU'RE OVER THE HILL WHEN...

You start reading the ads for hemorrhoids, constipation and hair loss remedies. Worse, you start buying the stuff.

YOU'RE OVER THE HILL WHEN...

Having sex is more like Thanksgiving than the 4th of July.

YOU'RE OVER THE HILL WHEN...

You have trouble finding your kind of music on the radio.

YOU'RE OVER THE HILL WHEN...

Sometimes you stop to think
and forget to start again.

YOU'RE OVER THE HILL WHEN...

All the prescriptions you never threw out overwhelm your medicine cabinet.

YOU'RE OVER THE HILL WHEN...

You can't remember when prunes, bran and figs weren't a regular part of your diet.

YOU'RE OVER THE HILL WHEN...

You keep forgetting. No matter how many calendars and appointment books you have you still forget. You write notes on slips of paper and then forget where you put the slips.

YOU'RE
OVER THE HILL
WHEN...

You no longer bounce checks.

YOU'RE OVER THE HILL WHEN...

You still pursue members of the opposite sex but you can't quite remember why.

YOU'RE
OVER THE HILL
WHEN...

Your bookshelf may be overflowing with
How To and Self Help books but you have
pretty well decided that you like yourself
just the way you are.

YOU'RE OVER THE HILL WHEN...

You stop looking forward to birthdays.
You plot revenge on people who give you
gifts like this book.